I'm Feeling...
JEALOUS

Published 2012 by
A&C Black
An imprint of Bloomsbury Publishing Plc
50 Bedford Square, London, WC1B 3DP

www.acblack.com
www.bloomsbury.com

ISBN 978-1-4081-7185-1

Copyright © 2012 Bloomsbury Publishing Plc
Text copyright © 2012 Lisa Regan

Illustrations: Christiane Engel
Series consultant: Sally Featherstone

This book is produced using paper that is made from
wood grown in managed, sustainable forests. It is natural,
renewable and recyclable. The logging and manufacturing
processes conform to the environmental regulations of the
country of origin.

Printed in China by C&C Offset Printer Co.

10 9 8 7 6 5 4 3 2 1

I'm Feeling...
JEALOUS

By Lisa Regan
Illustrated by Christiane Engel

It can be hard to feel happy all the time. Sometimes your friends have things that you want. Sometimes your parents have to share their time with you and their work, or your other family.

It's okay to feel jealous and wish everything happened the way you want. Read this book with a grown-up and talk about what makes you jealous. Try to remember that feeling bad inside doesn't make it okay to act mean, or be naughty.

Share your feelings and see if other people feel the same way. There's a big chance they do!

It can be hard when your brother has friends
round to play. You can feel left out.

If you can't join in their fun, make your own fun.
Spend some time with a parent, or work on
your own special project.

A new baby in the house can make everything feel different or strange. What if everyone loves the baby more than you?

Parents never run out of love for their children. You might have to share their time, but not their love.

Your big sister is invited to a sleepover at her friend's house. Why can't you do what she does?

Sometimes you have to wait until you are old enough
to try new things. It will be your turn one day!

Your friend Bella is chosen more often than you when your PE teacher wants a helper.

Don't hide at the back of the class. Make sure your teacher knows you want to help too.

Your best friend doesn't play with you as often these days. He has a new friend he plays with sometimes.

Try to make new friends so you have a big group of people to play with. Sometimes people like to have more than one friend.

Your big brother makes you feel sick. He's much better at swimming than you are.

Try to feel proud of your brother instead. He has had more practice than you because he's older. One day, you could be this good!

Zina is telling your teacher about her holiday. It makes you feel horrible because you're not going anywhere this year.

Try to feel happy for her and enjoy hearing her
holiday tales. Lots of people have holidays, but lots of
people stay at home too.

You've been playing at your friend's house with his brilliant building bricks. You feel like all your toys are just rubbish.

It's easy to get bored with the same toys and wish you had more. Why don't you get out some of the toys you haven't played with lately?

Notes for Parents and Caregivers

This series of books has been written to help you to help your child understand that strong feelings are a natural part of life, and that, with help from you, they can learn to manage their own feelings and responses to others.

Feeling Jealous is a book to share with your child. It is suitable for children from four years old, but you will still find it useful when your child is much older.

Strong feelings are a natural part of being human, and of developing relationships with others. Your child needs your help as he or she learns to manage their feelings without losing control or self-esteem. When your child feels cross, sad, shy, frustrated, angry, jealous or scared, you will understandably be concerned. But you don't have to wait until there is a crisis in your child's life or relationships before starting to help by reading this book - your child will be able to concentrate much better when they are calm.

Here are some general tips about using this book:

- Don't rush to read this book when your child is distressed. At this time they probably need a hug, a quiet time with you, or a favourite soft toy.

- For the first time, always read the book together, so your child understands what it is about. Then you can leave it for them to come back to in their own time.

- Choose a comfortable place, where you can sit together without being interrupted.

- Avoid distractions (TV, radio etc).

- Choose a calm and quiet time. Bedtime is ideal, as your child will be feeling relaxed, warm and comfy.

- If you have more than one child, read the book as a family. It's best not to single out one child. We all need help with managing our feelings, and brothers and sisters sometimes offer really helpful advice and comments.

- If your child seems bored or troubled by the book, stop and do something else. You could read a different book or talk about what you have been doing during the day.

Using this book

Here are some notes you could follow when reading this book with your child.

Read the title of the book, and look at the cover picture. Tell your child that the book is about feeling jealous, and check that they understand that being jealous or envious sometimes makes us want to be someone else or to have the things they have got. The children in this book are all feeling jealous, and need your child's help to stop wanting to be someone else. Even if your child hasn't ever felt jealous, it may help them to understand their friends or other children they meet.

Tell your child that everyone feels jealous sometimes, and this may make you feel cross or sad, or mad at someone else. All these responses are quite normal, even for grown-ups, and your child needs to know that there is nothing wrong with feeling a bit envious, but it helps to talk about what they could do when they feel envious themselves.

The first two pages of the book will help you to talk about feeling jealous, and some of the physical and emotional effects of this. Perhaps you could tell your child about a time when you felt envious, talk about how you felt and what you did.

The rest of the book describes some situations that can make children feel envious or jealous. As you look at each left hand page, before you read the words, see if your child can spot what is making the child in the book feel envious, and what is happening in the picture. Say "Who do you think is feeling jealous in this picture? How can you tell?"

Before you read the right hand page, ask your child how they could help the child by suggesting something they could do. Try to be positive about every suggestion, they may find it difficult at first, and older siblings might be able to help with ideas.

When you have finished reading the book, give your child a hug, tell them they are a good problem solver, and leave the book where they can return to it later.

Sally Featherstone